THE   BOOK   OF

# DIPS
## AND SALSAS

# THE BOOK OF
# DIPS
## AND SALSAS

### ELIZABETH WOLF-COHEN

Photography by
PATRICK McLEAVEY

HPBooks

ANOTHER BESTSELLING VOLUME FROM HPBOOKS

HPBooks
Published by The Berkley Publishing Group
A division of Penguin Putnam Inc.
375 Hudson Street
New York, New York 10014

Home Economist: Alison Austin

Notice: The information contained in this book is true and complete to
the best of our knowledge. All recommendations are made without any
guarantee on the part of the author or the publisher. The author and
the publisher disclaim all liability in connection with the use of this
information.

First edition: February 2000

The Penguin Putnam Inc. World Wide Web site address is
http://www.penguinputnam.com

This book has been cataloged with the Library of Congress.

ISBN 1-55788-341-6(tp)


Printed and bound in Spain

10   9   8   7   6   5   4   3   2   1

# CONTENTS

# FOREWORD

Dips are are simple tasty type of food that is easy to make, serve and eat. Although the appeal of salsas is more recent, they fall into the same category: strong, clean flavors and recipes that can be made quickly.

The variety of ingredients that can be used in both dips and salsas means that there is something for everyone. There are recipes for casual family gatherings, smart dinner parties, barbecues and picnics. Whatever your taste, these dishes will enhance your table.

*The Book of Dips and Salasa* includes recipes for old favorites such as Easy Clam Dip, Blue Cheese Dip and Chunky Guacamole alongside more fashionable combinations such as Thai Crab Dip, Mascarpone Pesto Dip (which is served with tortelloni dippers), Chili-lovers' Salsa, Spicy Mango Dip accompanied by fried wontons, and Pepper and Kumquat Relish.

Beautifully photographed recipes with easy to follow steps make each dish tantalizing and easy to prepare.

# INTRODUCTION

Dips and salsas are easy food - simple ingredients assembled with the minimum of bother, and tasty to eat. Salsas are often thought of as fresh 'new wave' cooking, and served as accompaniments to grilled (broiled) chicken, pork, fish or lamb. But they also make great dips; they are delicious with vegetables; make excellent alternative sandwich fillings; go really well with cheeses; and make great taco or pitta pocket fillings.

Dips have been found in various cultures around the world for many years, but it is the advent of the drinks party, a less formal version of a cocktail party, that popularized dips as they are known today. Because one hand usually held a glass, small pieces of food that could be eaten with the other hand were most popular. Savoury dips to accompany these foods were the natural offshoot.

Dips can be made very quickly, often from ingredients that are in the refrigerator or store cupboard, and they can often be made in advance. Usually the only last minute preparation that dips require is garnishing, which can be no more complicated than a fresh herb sprig or a sprinkling of a colourful spice such as paprika.

Dips are ideal for unexpected guests or when time is short. The introduction of early 'convenience' foods like packaged soup mixes, like onion soup mix combined with soured (sour) cream, is probably the first experience of the dip for most people. The blender, developed in the late 1930's, contributed the ability to puree fruits and vegetables easily.

Todays salsas have probably evolved from more complicated sauces because of the trend for lighter, simpler and less time consuming food preparation. Fast and tasty, salsas can be put together quickly and usually contain an overall spicy flavour combined with a little sweetness (from sugar or honey), sharpness (from lime or lemon juice, or vinegar) and an ingredient to add smoothness such as oil or fruit juice. The combinations vary and are as endless as the imagination, from avocados and bananas to watermelon and courgettes (zucchini). The best advice is to keep it easy, keep it fresh, and keep it zingy!

## TIPS FOR DIPS

Ideal bases for 'instant' dips are soured (sour) cream, yogurt, mayonnaise or cream cheese. Most people have one or more of these in their kitchen at any time, so can quickly make a dip by stirring a tablespoon or two of bottled pesto, chopped sun-dried tomatoes, olive paste (tapenade) or even just a handful of chopped fresh herbs into an instant base. A little ketchup (catsup) and prepared horseradish sauce stirred into mayonnaise makes the classic seafood sauce for prawns (shrimp) that is also great with raw vegetables. A spoonful of hot curry paste and some chutney or apple sauce stirred into plain yogurt is easy and tastes fantastic.

With a little extra time, more sophisticated dips with a special accompaniment can be made. Smoked Salmon and Dill Dip accompanied by cucumber sticks and bagel chips is always popular, while elegant Stilton Dip served with pear slices never fails to get rave reviews. Cheese Fondue with a selection of raw vegetables and breads for dipping makes is a great conversation piece.

Most dips benefit from being made in advance so that the flavours have a chance to blend; the exceptions are recipes that contain avocados, mushrooms, apples or bananas because they darken soon after cutting, while dips that include chopped juicy vegetables or fruits may give off too much liquid. Although hot dips should be served immediately, the preparation usually can be done in advance.

The texture of dips varies depending on the ingredients and the base; cream cheese and cheeses produce a stiff consistency whereas soured (sour) cream and yogurt are softer. The dips in this book vary; just remember to add any liquid gradually so you can stop when you get to the right texture – a good coating consistency is perfect. The dip shouldn't be so thin that it will drip on the carpet, or so thick that a knife is needed to spread it; remember, a little milk or liquid can be added to thin a dip that is too stiff. The calorie conscious can substitute the lower fat versions of these bases.

The number of people a dip will

serve depends on several factors. One dip served before a meal may disappear quickly; a party or buffet where there are several dips and other choices of canapes will not require such a large quantity. A rich dip may serve more people than a light one. How far a dip goes also depends on what is being dipped into it; toasts and breads are more filling than celery and carrot sticks. Use your own judgement and knowledge of your guests' tastes and appetites – one dip might serve 10 'ladies who lunch' but only four teenage boys with hearty appetites. It is always better to make extra – it never goes to waste but can be turned into a sandwich filling, spooned over vegetables and grilled (broiled) meats and fish, or turned into a salad dressing or sauce.

## WHAT TO DIP

There are no rules when it comes to choosing what to dip. Vegetables are ideal because they are easily handled and their crisp texture complements the softness of the dip. Choose any vegetables that you like as long as they can be eaten raw or lightly blanched. It is a good idea to match the flavours to the dip, but it's a personal choice. Carrots, celery, courgettes (zucchini), peppers (capsicum), fennel, and cucumbers cut into strips about 5cm (2 inches) long make the easiest choice. Stiff lettuce leaves, like Little Gem, Cos (romaine), radicchio and chicory (Belgian endive), make great little 'scoops'. Cauliflower and broccoli flowerettes, baby sweetcorn and asparagus tips benefit from light blanching: drop them into a saucepan of boiling water and simmer for 1-2 minutes, depending on the vegetable, then drain under cold running water until cool and pat dry with paper towels. Spring onions (scallions), radishes and slices of sweet onions such as Vadalia or Maui Maui are also tasty.

Some fruits make great dippers: pears, apples, nectarines and peaches darken fairly quickly so do not cut them too far in advance and dip them in a little lemon juice. Slices of melon, pineapple, mango and papaya, and strawberries, seedless grapes and clementine sections can also be good.

Potato chips were probably the first 'dippers' but today the range of 'dippable', ready-made snacks is almost endless. There must be something for every flavour and style of dip – tortilla chips, bread sticks, cheese straws, prawn (shrimp) and rice crackers. Breads of all kinds can be sliced, cut into cubes or sticks and toasted or fried to make croutons; pittas, bagels and other ethnic breads are ideal. Rye

and pumpernickel cocktail breads are available in packages.

For something more elaborate, batter-coated deep-fried prawns (shrimp), vegetable strips, or chicken, turkey or fish goujons are available pre-packaged, but you can easily make your own: sift 115g (4oz/1 cup) plain (all-purpose) flour into a large bowl, season with salt, freshly ground black pepper and a little paprika. Whisk in about 115ml (4fl oz/½ cup) beer until just blended (a few lumps don't matter). Dip into the batter large prawns (shrimp) or 2.5cm (1 inch) strips of chicken, turkey or vegetables and coat completely. Gently lower into a deep-fat fryer or large saucepan or wok of oil heated to 190C (375F) and fry for 1-2 minutes, depending on the food; chicken and turkey will take longer. Drain on paper towels.

Dips can be served in a kitchen bowl or a ramekin dish, but it is fun to display them in a more elaborate container. Try hollowing out a round loaf

of bread or small rolls, or making pretty containers from hollowed melon halves, pineapples, peppers (capsicums), tomatoes and patty pan squash; they make something simple look a little special.

## SUGGESTIONS FOR SALSAS

Salsas are generally easy to prepare. As most of the ingredients are fresh and colourful with a crunchy texture, they are best made no more than 2 hours ahead or just long enough to be chilled.

Many salsas contain chillies. How much you use is up to you. The recipes offer a guide, but if you like a very fiery flavour add more chillies, but remember the flavour will build up as more of the salsa is eaten.

Luckily salsas tend to be low in calories because they contain very little fat. The amount of oil can be decreased or even eliminated, but it does give a good texture and tends to pull the salsa together as a whole.

Fresh herbs are essential because they add intense flavours and colours. Don't be afraid to substitute one herb for another, or to increase the amount that is used: salsas are one kind of food that shouldn't be subtle.

Relishes and other condiments are similar to salsas, and are classic accompaniments. Some relishes are cooked, others are left raw to keep their flavours and colours fresh.

# TECHNIQUES

### Roasting Peppers (Capsicums)

1 Preheat the grill (broiler). Arrange the peppers (capsicums) on a foil-lined grill (broiler) pan or baking sheet and grill (broil) for 8-10 minutes until charred and blistered, turning frequently.

2 Transfer to a large plastic bag, twist to seal the top and leave until the peppers are cool enough to handle. Alternatively, push the peppers (capsicums) to the centre of the pan and cover with a large inverted bowl. The steam created helps to separate the skin from the flesh.

3 Using a sharp knife, peel off the charred skin and remove the stem and seeds. Cut the flesh into strips or chop, as the recipe directs, reserving any juices.

4 Chillies can be peeled in the same way, grilling (broiling) for slightly less time or closer to the heat source.

### Preparing Chillies

1 When handling chillies wear rubber, plastic or surgical gloves, because chillies contain a substance that can irritate the skin. Cut the chilli vertically in half.

2 Scrape out the stem and seeds (the seeds are the hottest part) and discard. Slice or chop as directed. Wash the cutting board, knife and gloves in hot soapy water.

### Peeling Tomatoes or Peaches

1 Over high heat, bring a large saucepan of water to the boil. With a small sharp knife, remove the stem end and score the bottom of the tomato or peach.

2 Gently lower 2-3 tomatoes or peaches into the water and leave for 30-60 seconds (depending on their ripeness); the skin will begin to curl off the flesh. Rinse under cold running water and drain.

3 Using a small sharp knife, or your fingertips, peel off the skins.

### Deseeding Tomatoes

Cut peeled tomatoes crosswise in half and either squeeze out the seeds and liquid, or use a spoon to scoop them out. Slice or chop as directed.

### Preparing Avocados

1 With a sharp knife, cut the avocado in half all round the fruit.

2 Twist the halves apart and remove the stone (pit) by striking with the blade of the knife and twisting out the stone (pit).

3 Using a spoon, scoop out the flesh and chop. Alternatively, run a blunt knife blade between the skin and flesh to loosen, then gently squeeze out the flesh and allow it to drop on to a work surface. Cut lengthwise into long slices or crosswise into half-moon shapes.

# BACON & EGG DIP

8oz (225g) bacon slices
1 cup (8oz/225g) cream cheese, softened
¼ cup (2fl oz/50ml) soured (sour) cream
2 hard-cooked eggs, peeled and finely chopped
2 scallions, finely chopped
2 tablespoons finely chopped fresh parsley
milk, for thinning (optional)
triangles of white and brown toast, to serve
plain savory crackers and raw vegetables (optional),
   to serve

In a medium skillet over a medium heat, cook bacon slices for 10 minutes until brown and crisp. Remove to paper towels to drain well.

In a medium bowl, beat together cream cheese and sour cream until smooth. Stir in hard-cooked eggs, scallions, and parsley until well blended. If mixture is too stiff, add a little milk to thin.

Crumble bacon and stir into dip, reserving 1 tablespoon bacon for garnish. Cover and refrigerate until required. About 15 minutes before serving, transfer dip to room temperature. Serve on toast triangles, sprinkled with reserved bacon. Alternatively, spoon into a serving bowl and arrange toast triangles, crackers, and raw vegetables around dip.

*Serves 6-8*

# —CHICKEN-CASHEW NUT DIP—

1 cup (4oz/115g) unsalted cashew nuts
6oz (175g) cooked boneless, skinless chicken breast,
  chopped
¾ cup (6fl oz/175ml) mayonnaise
¼ cup (2fl oz/50ml) sour cream
1-2 teaspoons soy sauce
½ teaspoon Asian sesame oil
salt and freshly ground black pepper
½ cup (2oz/50g) chopped celery
TO SERVE:
crusty bread
raw vegetables

Preheat oven to 375F (190C). Spread cashew nuts on a baking sheet and toast in oven for about 10 minutes until golden and fragrant, turning once or twice. (Alternatively, toast nuts over medium-low heat in a heavy-bottomed skillet for about 7 minutes until golden.) Pour on to a plate to cool, then chop.

In a food processor fitted with a metal blade, process chicken, mayonnaise, sour cream, soy sauce, sesame oil, salt, and plenty of pepper until smooth, scraping down the side of the bowl. Reserve 1 tablespoon cashew nuts. Stir remaining nuts and the celery into chicken mixture. Spoon into a serving dish, cover and refrigerate. About 15 minutes before serving, transfer dip to room temperature; sprinkle with reserved nuts and serve with the bread and vegetables.

*Serves 8-10*

## —— CHICKEN LIVER MOUSSE ——

1 cup (8oz/225g) plus 1 tablespoon unsalted butter, chopped
4-5 shallots OR 1 onion, finely chopped
1 clove garlic, crushed
1 fresh bay leaf
8oz (225g) chicken livers
1 sprig fresh thyme OR ½ teaspoon dried thyme
2 tablespoons brandy
salt and freshly ground black pepper
MELBA TOAST:
1 loaf medium-sliced bread

In a medium skillet over a medium heat, heat the 1 tablespoon butter until foaming. Add shallots or onion, garlic, and bay leaf and cook, stirring frequently, for about 5 minutes until shallots or onion are soft and translucent.

Increase heat to medium-high and add chicken livers and thyme; stir frequently for 5 minutes until livers are lightly browned but still pink inside. Add brandy and shake and stir for 30 seconds until evaporated. Add salt and pepper.

Remove bay leaf, and thyme sprig, if using, and pour liver mixture into a food processor fitted with a metal blade. Process until smooth, scraping down the side of the bowl once or twice.

With machine running, drop pieces of butter into liver mixture one at a time, allowing them to 'melt' in until all butter is absorbed. If liked, press through a strainer into a bowl. Pour mousse into a serving bowl or ramekins, or into a small loaf pan lined with plastic wrap. Cool and refrigerate until set.

To make Melba toast, heat broiler. Toast both sides of each slice of bread. Trim off crusts, making each slice square. Lay slices on a chopping board and, using a thin serrated knife, cut horizontally in half. Arrange, cut side up, on a baking sheet or broiler pan and toast for 1 minute until golden and edges curl. Leave to cool. Serve with mousse.

*Serves 10-12*

# ——— HAM & PINEAPPLE DIP ———

4oz (115g) lean, cooked ham slices
1 cup (8oz/225g) cottage cheese
8oz (225g) can pineapple pieces, drained and finely
   chopped, OR crushed pineapple in natural juice,
   well drained
freshly ground black pepper
½ cup (2oz/50g) Swiss cheese, chopped or grated
fresh mint, to garnish
TO SERVE:
sliced fruits such as apples, pears, mangoes and melon
raw vegetables

Chop ham; reserve 2 tablespoons.

In a food processor fitted with a metal blade,
process remaining ham and the cottage
cheese for about 15 seconds until smooth.
Add half pineapple, and pepper to food
processor. Using the pulse button, process
until just blended.

Scrape into a bowl and stir in remaining
pineapple, chopped or grated cheese, and
reserved chopped ham. Cover and
refrigerate until chilled. To serve dip, spoon
on to center of serving plate and surround
with fruit slices and raw vegetables of your
choice. Garnish with mint.

*Serves 6-8*

# TARAMASALATA

2 slices white bread, crusts removed
¼ cup (2fl oz/50ml) milk OR water
6-8oz (175-225g) smoked cod's roe
1 clove garlic, crushed
1 tablespoon grated onion (optional)
¾-1 cup (6-8fl oz/175-225ml) good quality olive oil
about ¼ cup (2fl oz/50ml) lemon juice
freshly ground black pepper
fresh parsley sprigs, to garnish
TO SERVE:
warm pita bread
large black Greek olives

Put bread in a medium bowl and pour milk or water over. Leave the bread to soak, then squeeze out excess liquid. Put bread into a food processor fitted with a metal blade. Add smoked cod's roe, garlic, and onion, if using, and process until smooth, scraping down the side of the bowl once or twice.

With the machine running, pour in olive oil in a thin stream until oil is absorbed and mixture is pale pink and creamy. Gradually add lemon juice to taste, pulsing to blend. Season with pepper. Scrape into a serving bowl, cover, and refrigerate until required. About 30 minutes before serving, transfer taramasalata to room temperature. Garnish with parsley and serve with pita bread and olives.

*Serves 4-6*

# BAGNA CAUDA

4 cloves garlic
¼ cup (2oz/50g) unsalted butter
¾-1 cup (6-8fl oz/175-225ml) extra-virgin olive oil
2oz (50g) can anchovy fillets
freshly ground black pepper
½-1 cup (4-8fl oz/115-225ml) heavy cream
  (optional)
TO SERVE:
a selection of raw and blanched vegetables
bread sticks
toasted ciabatta cubes
small cooked shrimp
ham cubes

Crush garlic and chop finely. In a small saucepan over a medium-low heat, melt butter in ¾ cup (6fl oz/175ml) olive oil.

Stir in garlic, and anchovies and their oil, crushing anchovies with the back of a spoon. Heat until mixture is warm and fragrant and anchovies are dissolved. Add remaining olive oil, and pepper. Gradually stir in cream if using. Transfer to a warmed fondue pot set over a lighted burner to keep warm. Serve immediately with fondue forks and accompaniments of your choice.

*Serves 6-8*

# ——— HOT CURRIED CRAB DIP ———

1 cup (8oz/225g) cream cheese, softened
½ cup (4fl oz/115ml) sour cream
2 scallions, finely chopped
1-2 teaspoons curry powder
2 tablespoons lemon juice
1 tablespoon chopped fresh dill OR parsley
8oz (225g) white crabmeat
milk, for thinning (optional)
3-4 tablespoons flaked or slivered almonds
TO SERVE:
crudités
toast

Preheat oven to 375F (190C). In a medium bowl, beat cream cheese with sour cream, scallions, curry powder, lemon juice, and dill or parsley until very smooth. Stir in crabmeat until just blended. If mixture is too stiff, add a little milk.

Spoon mixture into a gratin or baking dish and sprinkle with flaked or slivered almonds. Bake for about 15 minutes until top is golden and crab mixture is hot and bubbling. Serve immediately with crudités and toast.

*Serves 8-10*

# SMOKED TROUT MOUSSE

½ cup (4oz/115g) cream cheese
2 scallions, chopped
2 tablespoons chopped fresh dill OR parsley
1 teaspoon prepared horseradish
8oz (225g) smoked trout fillets, skinned, flaked, and
   fine bones removed
¼-½ cup (2-4fl oz/50-115ml) heavy cream
salt
few dashes hot pepper sauce
fresh dill sprigs, to garnish
1 cucumber, to serve

In a food processor fitted with a metal blade, process cream cheese, scallions, chopped dill or parsley, and horseradish until well blended. Add trout and process until smooth, scraping down the side of the bowl once or twice. With machine running, pour in cream until mixture is soft and creamy. Season with salt and hot pepper sauce. Scrape into a shallow serving bowl or plate, cover and refrigerate until required.

About 15 minutes before serving, transfer dip to room temperature. Using a cannelling knife or vegetable peeler, score along length of cucumber to create a striped effect. Cut cucumber crosswise into thin slices and arrange round dip. Garnish dip with dill sprigs and serve.

*Serves 6-8*

# TUNA-AVOCADO DIP

1 medium-large ripe avocado
¼ cup (2fl oz/50ml) mayonnaise
¼ cup (2fl oz/50ml) sour cream
2 tablespoons lime or lemon juice
1 tablespoon finely chopped scallion
2-3 dashes hot pepper sauce
2-3 dashes Worcestershire sauce
6½oz (190g) can tuna, well drained
1 tablespoon capers, coarsely chopped
1 tablespoon chopped fresh parsley OR cilantro
salt and freshly ground black pepper
fresh parsley OR cilantro, to garnish
CIABATTA STICKS:
1 black olive or plain ciabatta loaf
olive oil

Peel and mash avocado (see page 11). In a food processor fitted with a metal blade, process avocado, mayonnaise, sour cream, lime or lemon juice, scallion, hot pepper sauce, and Worcestershire sauce until smooth. Scrape mixture into a bowl and flake in tuna. Stir in capers, parsley or cilantro, and plenty of salt and pepper. Spoon into a serving dish, cover, and refrigerate.

To make ciabatta sticks, preheat oven to 375F (190C). With a serrated bread knife, slice ciabatta loaf horizontally in half. Brush cut side with olive oil, then cut bread lengthwise into ½in (1cm) strips. Place strips on a baking sheet. Bake for about 10 minutes until golden and crisp, turning once. About 15 minutes before serving, transfer dip to room temperature. Garnish with parsley or cilantro and serve with hot ciabatta strips.

*Serves 6-8*

## THAI CRAB DIP

2 stalks lemon grass, about 4in (10cm) long
4oz (115g) coconut cream
½ cup (4oz/115g) cream cheese
2 scallions, finely chopped
grated peel of 1 small lime
2 tablespoons lime juice
1 red chili, deseeded and finely chopped
1 tablespoon chopped fresh cilantro
freshly ground black pepper
6-8oz (175-225g) fresh or canned white crabmeat,
   well drained
fresh cilantro leaves, to garnish
TO SERVE:
shrimp crackers
scallions, strips red capsicum, strips cucumber, and
   celery sticks

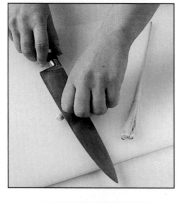

Lay lemon grass stalks on a chopping board and crush base of stems with flat of a large knife. In a small saucepan over a low heat, heat lemon grass and coconut cream for about 5 minutes until lemon grass flavor is released. Set aside to cool completely; strain, reserving coconut cream.

In a food processor fitted with a metal blade, process cream cheese, scallions, lime peel and juice, chili, and cilantro until smooth, scraping down the side of the bowl. With machine running, pour coconut cream into processor and process until well blended. Season with pepper and scrape into a serving bowl. Stir in crab, cover, and refrigerate until ready to serve. Garnish dip with cilantro leaves; serve with accompaniments.

*Serves 6-8*

# PINK SHRIMP DIP

1 cup (8fl oz/225ml) mayonnaise
¼ cup (2fl oz/50ml) chili sauce OR catsup
2-3 tablespoons lemon juice
1 tablespoon prepared horseradish sauce
1lb (450g) shelled cooked shrimp, coarsely chopped
TO SERVE:
crisp lettuce
celery sticks
cucumber sticks
Melba toast (see page 15)

In a small bowl, combine mayonnaise, chili sauce or catsup, lemon juice, and horseradish sauce.

Stir shrimp into mayonnaise mixture until blended. Spoon into a serving bowl, cover, and refrigerate until required.

Separate lettuce leaves and arrange on a plate with celery and cucumber sticks and Melba toast. Serve with dip.

*Serves 6-8*

# — SMOKED SALMON & DILL DIP —

8oz (225g) smoked salmon pieces or trimmings
1 cup (8oz/225g) cream cheese
grated peel of 1 small lemon
1 tablespoon lemon juice
1 cup (8fl oz/225ml) heavy cream
milk or extra cream, for thinning (optional)
2-3 tablespoons chopped fresh dill
2 scallions, finely chopped OR 2-3 tablespoons
  chopped fresh chives
freshly ground black pepper
TO SERVE:
crudités such as Belgian endive and celery
mini bagels, rye cocktail rounds, and pumpernickel
  bread

Chop smoked salmon.

In a food processor fitted with a metal blade, process smoked salmon, cream cheese, and lemon peel and juice until smooth, scraping down the side of the bowl once or twice. With machine running, gradually pour in cream until mixture is soft. If mixture is too stiff, add milk or a little extra cream to thin.

Add dill, scallions or chives, and pepper. Using pulse button, process to blend. Scrape into a serving bowl, cover, and refrigerate until required. Garnish with lemon peel and serve with crudités, mini bagels, rye cocktail rounds, and pumpernickel bread.

*Serves 8-10*

# - MEDITERRANEAN MAYONNAISE -

1¼ cups (10fl oz/300ml) mayonnaise
1 tablespoon Dijon mustard
1 tablespoon white wine vinegar or lemon juice
1 clove garlic, mashed
½-¾ cup (4-6 fl oz/115-175ml) extra-virgin olive oil
4-6 anchovy fillets, drained (if you like, add the oil to
  the mayonnaise)
1 tablespoon capers, roughly chopped
2 tablespoons freshly grated Parmesan cheese
3-4 tablespoons chopped fresh basil
¼ teaspoon cayenne pepper or to taste
TO SERVE:
strips of rare grilled (broiled) or roast beef
selection of salamis
chicory (Belgian endive) leaves and/or celery

In a food processor fitted with a metal blade, using pulse button, combine mayonnaise, mustard, vinegar or lemon juice, and garlic and process to blend, about 30 seconds (see top right). With the machine running, gradually add the oil in a thin steady stream until it is absorbed and the sauce is thickened and creamy. Add 1-2 tablespoons hot water and process to blend (this helps to prevent it separating if refrigerated).

In a small bowl, mash anchovy fillets. Add to the mayonnaise in the food processor with the capers, Parmesan, and basil, and season with cayenne. Using the pulse button, process to blend. Scrape into a serving bowl, cover, and refrigerate until required. About 15 minutes before serving, transfer dip to room temperature. Serve with accompaniments.

*Serves 8-10*

# EASY CLAM DIP

7oz (200g) can clams, drained
½ cup (4fl oz/115ml) mayonnaise
½ cup (4fl oz/115ml) sour cream OR plain yogurt
2-3 tablespoons lemon juice
2 tablespoons finely chopped fresh parsley
2 tablespoons finely chopped scallions
1 teaspoon Worcestershire sauce
freshly ground black pepper
fresh parsley, to garnish
TO SERVE:
plain savory crackers
crudités

Dry clams on paper towels. In a medium bowl, beat mayonnaise and sour cream or yogurt until smooth.

Stir in lemon juice, parsley, and scallions. Stir clams into mayonnaise mixture, then season with Worcestershire sauce and pepper. Spoon into a serving bowl, cover, and refrigerate until required. Garnish with parsley and serve with plain savory crackers and crudités.

*Serves 6-8*

# STILTON DIP

8oz (225g) mature blue Stilton cheese, at room
  temperature
¾ cup (6oz/175g) medium- or low-fat cream cheese,
  at room temperature
2 scallions, chopped
freshly ground black pepper
1 cup (8fl oz/225ml) heavy cream
milk, for thinning
2 or more ripe red, green, and yellow dessert pears, to
  serve

In a bowl and using a fork, mash Stilton. In
a food processor fitted with a metal blade,
mix Stilton, cream cheese, scallions, and
pepper until blended.

Scrape down bowl of mixer and add cream
in one go; process until smooth, scraping
down bowl again. If mixture is too stiff,
gradually add some milk to soften it to a
dipping consistency. Scrape into a serving
bowl, swirling the surface to create an
attractive design. Cover and refrigerate.

About 30 minutes before serving, garnish
dip with black pepper and leave at room
temperature. Quarter, core, and thinly slice
pears. Arrange alternating slices of pear
colors around dip or in an attractive pattern
and serve.

*Serves 6-8*

**TIP:** This makes a delicious sandwich
spread if fairly thick; just add enough cream
and milk to make a spreading consistency.

# ── GOATS' CHEESE & HERB DIP ──

8oz (225g) soft goats' cheese logs, at room
  temperature
⅓ cup (3oz/85g) low-fat cream cheese, at room
  temperature
½ cup (4fl oz/115ml) plain Greek yogurt
4 tablespoons finely chopped fresh herbs such as chives,
  parsley, oregano, cilantro, dill, or mint
12 large, black Greek olives, pitted and chopped
  (optional)
salt and freshly ground black pepper
TO SERVE:
pita bread
cherry tomatoes and crudités

Remove rind from goats' cheese.

In a food processor fitted with a metal blade,
process goats' cheese, cream cheese, and
yogurt for about 1 minute until smooth and
creamy, scraping down bowl once or twice.
Add herbs, olives, if using, and season with
salt and pepper; pulse once or twice until
just blended.

Scrape dip into a serving dish and smooth
the top. Cover and refrigerate until
required. About 15 minutes before serving,
transfer dip to room temperature. Preheat
broiler. Toast pita bread then cut into strips.
Arrange around dip, with cherry tomatoes
and crudités, and serve immediately.

*Serves 6-8*

**TIP:** Goats' cheeses vary in softness, so if
dip is too stiff add a little more yogurt or
milk to soften to a dipping consistency.

# —— DILLED CREAM CHEESE DIP ——

1 cup (8oz/225g) cream cheese
¼ cup (2fl oz/50ml) mayonnaise
¼ cup (2fl oz/50ml) milk
½ teaspoons chopped aniseeds
3-4 tablespoons chopped fresh dill
salt and freshly ground black pepper
1 teaspoon lemon juice
2 large fennel bulbs, feathery tops reserved, to serve

In a medium bowl and using a wooden spoon, beat cream cheese to soften. Blend in mayonnaise, then beat in milk until mixture is smooth and creamy.

In a small bowl, using the back of a wooden spoon, lightly crunch aniseeds to release the flavor, then stir into dip with dill. Season with salt, pepper, and lemon juice. Spoon into a serving bowl, cover, and refrigerate until ready to serve.

About 15 minutes before serving, transfer dip to room temperature. Slice fennel bulbs lengthwise in half. With a sharp knife, remove triangular core. Cut each bulb half into long strips. Sprinkle reserved fennel tops over dip and serve accompanied by the fennel strips.

*Serves 4-6*

# — SZECHUAN PEPPERCORN DIP —

2 tablespoons Szechuan peppercorns
1 cup (8oz/225g) cream cheese, softened
¼ cup (2oz/50g) silken tofu
2 tablespoons Chinese plum sauce
1 tablespoon Asian sesame oil
1 tablespoon sesame seeds, lightly toasted
TO SERVE:
shrimp
asparagus
baby sweetcorn

In a small skillet over a medium heat, heat peppercorns for about 1 minute until they begin to release their fragrance, stirring frequently. Remove from heat to cool.

In a medium bowl, beat cream cheese. Gradually beat in tofu, then plum sauce, and oil until smooth.

Pour cooked peppercorns into a small plastic bag and roll a rolling pin over them gently to crush coarsely. Stir into dip. Transfer to a serving dish, cover, and refrigerate until required. About 15 minutes before serving, transfer dip to room temperature. Sprinkle with toasted sesame seeds and serve with shrimp, asparagus, and baby sweetcorn.

*Serves 4-6*

# CHEESE FONDUE

2 cups (8oz/225g) Swiss cheese
2 cups (8oz/225g) Emmenthal cheese
1¼ cups (10fl oz/300ml) dry white wine
1 large clove garlic, lightly crushed
2 teaspoons cornstarch
2 tablespoons kirsch or other unsweetened cherry
  brandy
freshly ground black pepper
TO SERVE:
crusty French or Italian bread, cubed
sesame bread sticks
spicy cured sausage, cut into pieces
small pickled onions or blanched vegetables such as
  cauliflower or broccoli

Grate cheeses.

In a large heavy-based saucepan over a low heat, heat wine and garlic for about 2 minutes until garlic flavors the wine. Discard garlic. Add cheeses to wine. Heat very gently for 15-20 minutes until cheese is melted and smooth, stirring frequently.

Put cornstarch into a small dish or cup and stir in kirsch until dissolved. Stir into melted cheese, blending completely. Season with pepper to taste and transfer to a warmed fondue pot. Set over a lighted burner to keep warm. Serve immediately with fondue forks and accompaniments.

*Serves 6-8*

**TIP:** Take care to melt the cheeses very slowly otherwise they will separate and become grainy in texture.

# MEXICAN CHEESE DIP

2 jalapeño chilies OR 3-4 tablespoons pickled
   jalapeños, chopped
1½ tablespoons vegetable oil
1 onion, finely chopped
1 teaspoon cornstarch
1 cup (8fl oz/225ml) sour cream
2 cups (8oz/225g) grated Monterey Jack or mature
   Cheddar cheese
1 scallion, finely chopped
tortilla chips, to serve

Hold fresh chilies one at a time over a gas flame, turning until skin begins to bubble and blacken evenly. Alternatively, place chilies on a baking sheet and broil until skin bubbles and blackens, turning frequently. Place chilies in a plastic bag and seal until cool enough to handle. Remove from bag. Wearing rubber gloves, peel or rinse away charred skin. Discard seeds and chop finely; set aside.

In a medium saucepan over a medium heat, heat the oil. Add onion and cook until softened and just beginning to color. Stir in chilies and cook for 1-2 minutes longer. Stir in cornstarch until well blended. Gradually stir in sour cream and reduce heat; do not allow to boil. Add cheese and stir frequently until melted and smooth. Pour into a heatproof bowl, sprinkle with chopped scallion, and serve with tortilla chips.

*Serves 4-6*

# —BROILED BRIE WITH PECANS—

1 tablespoon unsalted butter, softened
1 teaspoon Dijon mustard
1-2 dashes hot pepper sauce
8in (20cm) wheel of brie cheese
¼ cup (1oz/25g) chopped pecans, walnuts, or
  almonds
1 teaspoon light brown sugar (optional)
TO SERVE:
toasted French bread
bread sticks
skewered ham cubes
crudités

Preheat broiler. In a small bowl, combine butter, mustard, and hot pepper sauce to taste and spread evenly over top of brie cheese. Place cheese on a heatproof serving plate or broiler pan and broil about 6in (15cm) from heat for 3-4 minutes until top just begins to bubble.

Sprinkle surface of cheese with chopped nuts, and brown sugar, if liked. Broil for 2-3 minutes longer until topping is golden and nuts and sugar begin to caramelize and cheese is bubbling. Remove to a wire rack to cool slightly. If necessary slide on to a warmed serving dish. Serve cheese immediately with accompaniments of your choice.

*Serves 10-12*

## —— MASCARPONE PESTO DIP ——

½ cup (4oz/115g) mascarpone OR cream cheese
¼ cup (1oz/25g) toasted pine nuts (see page 57)
½ cup (2oz/50g) freshly grated Parmesan cheese
2 cups (2oz/50g) fresh basil
1 clove garlic, chopped
salt and freshly ground black pepper
milk, for thinning
TO SERVE:
1lb (450g) fresh cheese-filled tortelloni
olive oil

In a food processor fitted with a metal blade, process mascarpone or cream cheese, pine nuts, Parmesan, basil, garlic, salt, and pepper until well blended, scraping down bowl occasionally. Add enough milk to obtain a dipping consistency. Scrape into a serving bowl. Cover and refrigerate. Bring a large saucepan of lightly salted water to the boil. Add tortelloni and cook for about 10 minutes until tender, or according to package directions. Drain, refresh under running cold water, tip into a bowl and toss with olive oil. Cover until required.

Using 6in (15cm) wooden skewers, thread 1 tortelloni on to each skewer and arrange on a plate with all the skewers facing the same direction, or in a circle. Serve at room temperature with dip.

*Serves 10-12*

# BLUE CHEESE DIP

1 cup (4oz/115g) blue cheese such as Roquefort or
  Danish Blue, softened
½ cup (4fl oz/115ml) sour cream
½ cup (4fl oz/115ml) mayonnaise
2 tablespoons chopped fresh chives
2 tablespoons chopped fresh celery leaves
freshly ground black pepper
TO SERVE:
1 head celery
good quality walnut halves

In a bowl, mash blue cheese. Slowly beat in
sour cream and mayonnaise until smooth
and creamy. Stir in chives and celery leaves
and season with black pepper. Spoon into a
serving bowl. Cover and refrigerate until
required.

About 30 minutes before serving, transfer
dip to room temperature. Separate celery
sticks. Using a vegetable peeler, peel outside
edge of each celery stick to remove strings.
Rinse well and cut each celery stick
lengthwise in half then into 3-4in
(7.5-10cm) pieces. Place dip on a serving
plate and arrange the celery sticks and
walnut halves around.

*Serves 6-8*

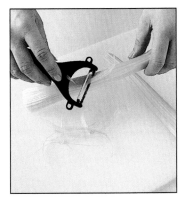

# — SMOKED CHEESE & ONION DIP —

1 small sweet, mild onion
1 cup (8oz/225g) smoked cheese, chopped
1 cup (8fl oz/225ml) plain or herb mayonnaise
1 teaspoon Dijon mustard
freshly ground black pepper
paprika, to garnish
TO SERVE:
cucumber wedges
green capsicum strips
cheese crackers

Chop onion very finely; reserve
1 tablespoon.

In a food processor fitted with a metal blade,
process onion, cheese, mayonnaise, mustard,
and pepper to taste until smooth, scraping
down the side of the bowl once or twice.
Add reserved onion and pulse once or twice
until just blended. Scrape into a serving
bowl, cover, and refrigerate for 24 hours, or
until ready to serve.

About 30 minutes before serving, transfer
dip to room temperature to soften. Dust top
with paprika and serve with cucumber
wedges, green capsicum strips, and cheese
crackers.

*Serves 6-8*

# CHEDDAR-BEER DIP

225g (8oz) sharp Cheddar cheese
225g (8oz) Monterey Jack cheese, or additional
  Cheddar cheese
2 cloves garlic, finely chopped
2-3 tablespoons hot or mild chili sauce
1 teaspoon dry mustard powder
¾ cup (6fl oz/175ml) good quality beer
TO SERVE:
scallions
cucumber sticks
plain savory crackers
cocktail rye rounds
pumpernickel bread

Cut cheeses into cubes. Using a food processor fitted with a metal blade, process cheeses, garlic, chili sauce, and mustard until smooth.

With machine running, slowly add beer until mixture is smooth and creamy. Scrape into a bowl, cover, and refrigerate until required. About 15 minutes before serving, transfer dip to room temperature. Arrange scallions, cucumber sticks, savory crackers, cocktail rye rounds, and pumpernickel bread around dip.

*Serves 10-12*

**TIP:** To serve warm: microwave on High (100% power) for about 10 seconds.

# ─── SMOKY EGGPLANT DIP ───

1 large eggplant
50ml (2fl oz/¼ cup lemon juice
3-4 cloves garlic, crushed
3-4 tablespoons sesame seed paste OR mayonnaise
salt and freshly ground black pepper
2-4 tablespoons olive oil
2 tablespoons chopped fresh parsley
TO SERVE:
crudités
warm pita bread

Preheat broiler to medium. Place eggplant on a baking sheet and pierce with a knife in several places.

Broil eggplant for about 30 minutes until well charred on all sides, turning frequently. Allow to cool. Cut  lengthwise in half and scoop flesh into a food processor fitted with a metal blade. Add lemon juice, garlic, sesame seed paste or mayonnaise, and salt and pepper. Process until smooth, scraping down bowl once or twice.

With machine running, slowly add olive oil until mixture is smooth and very creamy. Reserve 1 tablespoon parsley and add remaining parsley to food processor. Using pulse button, process until well blended. Spoon into a serving bowl, cover and refrigerate until ready to serve. Garnish with remaining parsley and serve with a selection of crudités and warm pita bread.

*Serves 6-8*

# TZATZIKI

1 large cucumber
1 teaspoon salt
2½ cups (20fl oz/550ml) Greek-style yogurt
2-3 cloves garlic, crushed
3-4 tablespoons chopped fresh mint
1-2 tablespoons olive oil (optional)
paprika OR cayenne pepper, for sprinkling
mint sprigs, to garnish
2-3 large pita breads, to serve

Peel cucumber and cut lengthwise into quarters. Scrape out seeds and chop very finely. Put cucumber into a colander over a plate and sprinkle with salt. Allow to drain for about 1 hour. Pat dry with paper towels.

Put yogurt in a large bowl and stir in cucumber, garlic, and mint. Blend in the olive oil, if using. Spoon into a serving dish, cover and refrigerate until ready to serve.

Just before serving, sprinkle tzatziki with paprika or cayenne, and add a sprig of mint. Preheat broiler. Cut each pita bread lengthwise in half, then cut each half into triangles. Arrange on a baking sheet and broil for about 3 minutes, turning once, until crisp and golden. Serve immediately with dip.

*Serves 10-12*

# – SUN-DRIED TOMATO-BASIL DIP –

1 tablespoon pine nuts
3oz (85g) sun-dried tomatoes in olive oil
½ cup (4oz/115g) mascarpone cheese OR cream
  cheese
½ cup (4fl oz/115ml) cup mayonnaise
2 cloves garlic, crushed
1 tablespoon balsamic vinegar
2-3 tablespoons oil from sun-dried tomatoes
1 tablespoon chopped fresh oregano OR marjoram
2 tablespoons fresh basil, torn into pieces
fresh basil leaves, to garnish
TO SERVE:
red, yellow, and green capsicum strips
ciabatta sticks (see page 21) and/or garlic bread

Toast pine nuts for 5 minutes (see page 57).

Coarsely chop sun-dried tomatoes. Put into a food processor fitted with a metal blade. Add mascarpone cheese or cream cheese, mayonnaise, garlic, balsamic vinegar, and sun-dried tomato oil. Process until nearly smooth and scrape down bowl of processor.

Add oregano and basil and process until smooth, scraping down bowl again. If mixture is too thick, add a little more of the oil, or boiling water. Spoon into a serving bowl, cover, and refrigerate. About 15 minutes before serving, transfer dip to room temperature. Sprinkle with the toasted pine nuts and garnish with basil leaves. Serve with accompaniments.

*Serves 6-8*

# — SQUASH & PARMESAN DIP —

2lb (1kg) butternut squash or piece of pumpkin, cut
  into wedges and deseeded
1 yellow capsicum, quartered and deseeded
2 tablespoons olive oil, plus extra for brushing
1 onion, chopped
2 cloves garlic, crushed
½ teaspoon dried thyme
¼ cup (1oz/25g) freshly grated Parmesan cheese
salt and freshly ground black pepper
¼ cup (1oz/25g) pumpkin seeds OR pine nuts
TO SERVE:
ciabatta sticks (see page 21)
garlic bread or bread sticks

Preheat oven to 375F (190C). Halve squash
and scoop out seeds. Put squash or pumpkin
and capsicum on to a baking sheet and
brush generously with olive oil. Roast for
about 45 minutes until flesh is tender and
edges are just beginning to char, turning
occasionally. Remove to a heatproof surface
to cool slightly. When squash or pumpkin is
cool enough to handle, scoop flesh from
rind into a food processor fitted with a metal
blade. Add yellow capsicum quarters.

In a skillet over a medium heat, heat olive
oil. Add onion and cook for about 5
minutes until beginning to soften. Add
garlic and thyme and cook for 4-5 minutes
until mixture is soft and golden. Remove
from heat to cool. Add to food processor and
process until smooth, scraping down bowl.
Add Parmesan, salt, and pepper. Pulse to
blend. Scoop into a serving bowl and
sprinkle with pumpkin seeds or pine nuts.
Serve warm with accompaniments.

*Serves 8-10*

# — LOW-FAT WATERCRESS DIP —

4oz (115g) watercress
1 cup (8fl oz/225ml) low-fat Greek or thick yogurt
   OR ½ cup (4fl oz/115ml) yogurt and ½ cup (4fl oz/
   115ml) reduced calorie mayonnaise, mixed
freshly ground black pepper
lemon juice
2 large slices smoked salmon
1lb (450g) cooked large shrimp
lemon wedge to serve

Cut coarse stems from watercress. Reserve a few watercress sprigs for garnish.

Put remaining watercress in a food processor fitted with a metal blade, add yogurt and, if using, mayonnaise. Season with pepper and a little lemon juice. Process until smooth, scraping down bowl once or twice. Scrape into a bowl, cover, and refrigerate until required.

Spread salmon slices on work surface. Sprinkle with a little pepper and lemon juice. Cut slices lengthwise into 1½in (4cm) strips about 4in (10cm) long. Roll each strip into a log shape. Arrange smoked salmon rolls and shrimp on a plate and garnish with watercress sprigs. About 15 minutes before serving, transfer dip to room temperature. Garnish with another watercress sprig and serve with smoked salmon rolls and shrimp.

*Serves 4-6*

# TAPENADE DIP

1 cup (6oz/175g) Kalamata or other good quality
  black olives, pitted
1-2 cloves garlic, crushed
1 tablespoon capers, rinsed and drained
3-4 tablespoons virgin olive oil, plus extra to serve
  (optional)
2-4 anchovy fillets, drained
2-3 tablespoons freshly squeezed lemon juice
freshly ground black pepper
pinch ground ginger
¼ teaspoon freshly grated nutmeg
pinch ground cloves
1-2 tablespoons finely chopped fresh parsley
TO SERVE:
toasted ciabatta or Italian bread
selection of crudités

Reserve 1 olive to garnish. Put remaining
olives into a food processor fitted with a
metal blade and add remaining ingredients,
except parsley. Process until smooth and
well blended but mixture retains some
texture.

Add parsley and, using pulse button, process
until just blended. Spoon into a serving
bowl, cover, and refrigerate until required.
About 15 minutes before serving, transfer to
room temperature. Drizzle with a little olive
oil if liked and garnish with reserved black
olive. Serve with toasted bread and crudités.

*Serves 6-8*

**TIP:** For a milder flavor, stir in a mixture of
mascarpone and cream cheese or crème
fraîche, to taste.

# WARM ARTICHOKE DIP

2 x 13oz (375g) cans artichoke hearts in brine,
  drained
1 cup (8fl oz/225ml) garlic-flavored mayonnaise
2 scallions, finely chopped
1-2 tablespoons lemon juice
1 cup (4oz/115g) freshly grated Parmesan cheese,
  plus extra for sprinkling
2 tablespoons chopped fresh parsley
½ teaspoon dried thyme
½ teaspoon dried oregano
cayenne pepper
paprika or mild chili powder, to garnish
toasted French bread, to serve

Preheat oven to 350F (180C). Lightly oil a
1 quart (40fl oz/1 litre) shallow baking dish.
Dry artichokes on paper towels; cut any
large artichoke hearts into halves or
quarters. Mix with mayonnaise, scallions,
lemon juice, Parmesan cheese, parsley,
thyme, and oregano, and cayenne pepper to
taste.

Spread artichoke mixture evenly in baking
dish and sprinkle with a little Parmesan
cheese and paprika or chili powder. Bake for
about 20 minutes until hot and lightly
browned on top. Serve immediately with
toasted French bread.

*Serves 6-8*

# —RED CAPSICUM & PINE NUT DIP—

2 large red capsicums
3-4 tablespoons olive oil
1-2 red chilies, pierced
2 unpeeled cloves garlic, lightly crushed
1 teaspoon light brown sugar
1 teaspoon balsamic vinegar
¾ cup (6oz/175g) cream cheese OR mascarpone
  cheese OR ½ cream cheese and ½ mascarpone
  cheese
2-3 tablespoons thick plain yogurt OR mayonnaise
2 tablespoons chopped fresh cilantro
2 tablespoons pine nuts, lightly toasted (see page 57)
TO SERVE:
crudités
selection of crispbreads, or toast

Preheat oven to 400F (200C). Put capsicums in a baking dish and brush generously with olive oil on all sides. Bake for 15 minutes. Oil chilies and add to capsicums, with cloves garlic. Bake for 15-20 minutes longer until skins are blistered and beginning to char. Remove capsicums, chilies, and garlic to a large plastic bag and twist to seal. When cool enough to handle, peel capsicums, chilies, and garlic then discard the stems, seeds, and any membranes.

Put capsicums, chilies, and garlic in a food processor fitted with a metal blade and process until smooth, scraping down bowl. Add sugar and vinegar and, using pulse button, process to blend. Add cream cheese and yogurt and process until smooth. Spoon into a serving dish, stir in cilantro, cover, and refrigerate. About 20 minutes before serving, transfer to room temperature. Sprinkle with pine nuts and serve with accompaniments.

*Serves 4-6*

# ASPARAGUS DIP

2lb (1kg) fresh asparagus
½ cup (4fl oz/115ml) heavy cream, whipped
½ cup (4fl oz/115ml) mayonnaise
1-2 tablespoons lemon juice
freshly ground black pepper

Bring a large, deep skillet filled with 3in (7.5cm) of water to the boil. Strip any coarse skin from base of asparagus stems, if necessary. Add asparagus to pan and return to boil. Lower heat to medium and simmer for about 5 minutes until spears are tender when pierced with a sharp knife. Drain and rinse asparagus under running cold water.

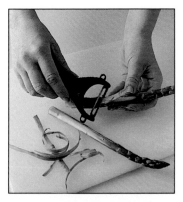

Lay on several thicknesses of paper towels and pat dry with more towels. Cut asparagus crosswise in half, leaving tip end about 4in (10cm) long. Arrange tips on a serving dish. Cover and refrigerate.

Coarsely chop remaining stems and put into a food processor fitted with a metal blade. Process until as smooth as possible, scraping down bowl once or twice. (Add a little of the cream if necessary.) In a medium bowl, fold cream into mayonnaise. Add lemon juice and puréed asparagus. Season with pepper. Scrape into a serving bowl, cover and refrigerate until ready to serve, accompanied by the chilled asparagus tips.

*Serves 4-6*

# CHUNKY GUACAMOLE

2 ripe avocados, mashed (see page 11)
juice of 1 small lime
2 tablespoons chopped red onion
½ teaspoon ground cumin (optional)
1 ripe tomato, peeled, deseeded, and chopped (see
  page 11)
1-2 jalapeño chilies, peeled, deseeded, and finely
  chopped (see page 11)
salt
2-4 tablespoons chopped fresh cilantro
sour cream, to garnish
TO SERVE:
4 corn tortillas
vegetable oil, for frying

In a bowl and using a fork, mix together avocado and lime juice. Add onion, cumin, if using, tomato, jalapeño, and salt to taste. Stir in cilantro. Spoon into a serving bowl, cover, and refrigerate until ready to serve. Place tortillas on a work surface and cut into 3 lengths. Cut each length into rough triangle shapes. Over a medium heat, heat a saucepan containing 2in (5cm) vegetable oil. When very hot, carefully add several tortilla triangles and fry for about 1 minute, turning until crisp and brown.

Using a slotted spoon, remove tortilla chips to paper towels to drain. Continue frying and draining tortilla triangles, a few at a time. Garnish dip with a spoonful of sour cream and serve with tortilla chips.

*Serves 4-6*

**TIP:** Pickled jalapeño chilies are available in jars from most supermarkets. If preferred, fresh chilies can be used.

# SPINACH & EGG DIP

6 eggs, hard-cooked, peeled
1lb (450g) fresh spinach, cooked, squeezed dry, and
  finely chopped
1 cup (8fl oz/225ml) mayonnaise
½ cup (4fl oz/115ml) sour cream
4 tablespoons chopped fresh chives OR scallions
2 tablespoons chopped fresh parsley
2 tablespoons chopped fresh dill
1 tablespoon Dijon mustard
salt and freshly ground black pepper
TO SERVE:
red, yellow and green capsicum strips
cocktail-size crackers or rye and pumpernickel bread
  fingers

Finely chop eggs. Put into a large bowl and stir in spinach, mayonnaise, sour cream, chives or scallions, parsley, dill, mustard, salt, and pepper; the mixture should be soft but hold its shape.

Spoon spinach and egg mixture into a serving dish. Serve dip with capsicum strips, crackers, and bread fingers.

*Serves 8-10*

# PEA GUACAMOLE

10oz (300g) frozen peas, thawed and drained
¼ cup (2fl oz/50ml) mayonnaise
2 scallions, chopped
1 clove garlic, crushed
1 jalapeño chili, deseeded and finely chopped
2-3 tablespoons lime OR lemon juice
1 tablespoon vegetable oil
milk, for thinning (optional)
salt and freshly ground pepper
2-3 tablespoons chopped fresh mint
mint sprigs, to garnish
selection of raw vegetables, to serve

Remove 1 tablespoon peas and chop coarsely; set aside.

Put remaining peas into a food processor fitted with a metal blade. Add mayonnaise, scallions, garlic, jalapeño, lime or lemon juice, and oil and process until smooth, scraping down bowl once or twice. If mixture is too stiff, gradually add some milk and process until creamy and smooth. Season to taste with salt and pepper.

Spoon into a serving bowl, stir in mint, cover, and refrigerate until required. About 30 minutes before serving, transfer dip to room temperature. Sprinkle with reserved chopped peas and garnish with mint sprigs. Serve with raw vegetables.

*Serves 4-6*

# SPANISH GARLIC DIP

2 unpeeled heads garlic, separated into cloves
3 tablespoons olive oil
½ cup (4fl oz/115ml) mayonnaise
½ cup (4fl oz/115ml) sour cream OR thick plain
   yogurt
1 teaspoon mild, sweet mustard
salt and freshly ground black pepper
TO SERVE:
selection of capsicum strips and other Mediterranean
   vegetables such as zucchini and fennel
bread sticks
French bread

Preheat oven to 350F (180C). Put garlic cloves into a small roasting pan and drizzle with olive oil. Toss well to coat evenly. Bake for 35-40 minutes until very tender when pierced with the tip of a knife, stirring occasionally. Transfer garlic to a plate or chopping board to cool slightly. When cool enough to handle, squeeze each garlic clove out of its skin (most of the skins will have split - if not use a knife to open), on to a chopping board. Using a small knife, chop and crush garlic on board until very smooth. Transfer to a bowl.

Gradually beat mayonnaise into garlic, then stir in sour cream or yogurt, and mustard. Season lightly with salt and pepper. Spoon into a serving bowl, cover, and refrigerate until required. About 30 minutes before serving, transfer dip to room temperature then serve with accompaniments.

*Serves 4-6*

## BEET DIP

8oz (225g) cooked natural beets (not in vinegar), cut
 into chunks
½ cup (4oz/115g) cream cheese
½-¾ cup (4-6fl oz/115ml-175ml) sour cream
2 tablespoons chopped fresh dill
salt and freshly ground black pepper
1-2 tablespoons chopped walnuts or pecans
crudités, to serve

Put beets into chunks into a food processor
fitted with a metal blade. Using pulse
button, process until finely chopped,
scraping down side of bowl once or twice.
Spoon about one third of the chopped beets
into a medium bowl and set aside.

Add the cream cheese to beets in food
processor and process until mixture is
smooth, scraping down side of bowl once or
twice. Scrape into the bowl with reserved
beets. Add half sour cream and stir until
well blended.

Add remaining sour cream, a tablespoon at
a time, until smooth and just soft enough to
hold its shape. Stir in chopped dill and
season to taste with salt and pepper. Scrape
into a serving bowl, cover and refrigerate
until ready to serve. Place the dip in the
center of a serving platter and sprinkle with
chopped walnuts or pecans. Arrange
crudités around bowl and serve.

*Serve 8-10*

## HUMMUS

18oz (500g) can garbanzos, drained and liquid
  reserved
¼ cup (2oz/50g) sesame seed paste
¼ cup (2fl oz/50ml) lemon juice
2-3 cloves garlic, crushed
salt
cayenne pepper
2-3 tablespoons olive oil
2 tablespoons chopped fresh parsley or cilantro
TO SERVE:
crudités
hot pita bread

Finely chop about 2 tablespoons garbanzos and set aside.

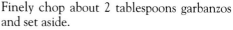
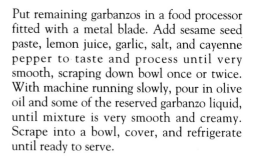

Put remaining garbanzos in a food processor fitted with a metal blade. Add sesame seed paste, lemon juice, garlic, salt, and cayenne pepper to taste and process until very smooth, scraping down bowl once or twice. With machine running slowly, pour in olive oil and some of the reserved garbanzo liquid, until mixture is very smooth and creamy. Scrape into a bowl, cover, and refrigerate until ready to serve.

To serve, stir well and spoon into a shallow serving dish. Using the back of a tablespoon, create a well in the dip. Pour in a little olive oil, add reserved chopped garbanzos, and sprinkle with a little cayenne pepper and the parsley or cilantro. Serve with crudités and hot pita bread.

*Serve 4-6*

# FIERY CHILI BEAN DIP

2 red or green chilies
15oz (425g) can red kidney beans, drained and liquid
   reserved
2-3 cloves garlic, crushed
1 small onion, finely chopped
juice 1 small lime
pinch ground cumin
6oz (175g) can sweetcorn kernels, drained
2 tablespoons vegetable oil
2 tablespoons chopped fresh cilantro
TO GARNISH:
sour cream
grated Monterey Jack or Cheddar cheese
TO SERVE:
red, green, and yellow capsicum strips
tortilla chips

Deseed and finely chop chilies (see page 11). In a food processor fitted with a metal blade, process chilies, beans, garlic, onion, lime juice, and cumin until very smooth, scraping down bowl once or twice. If mixture is too stiff add some of the reserved bean liquid to thin to a dipping consistency.

Scrape dip into a bowl and stir in sweetcorn kernels, oil, and cilantro. Spoon into a serving dish, cover, and refrigerate until required. About 30 minutes before serving, transfer dip to room temperature. Spoon a little sour cream on top and sprinkle with grated cheese. Serve with capsicum strips and tortilla chips.

*Serves 6-8*

## CURRIED DHAL

2 tablespoons sunflower oil
1 onion, finely chopped
2-3 cloves garlic, crushed
1in (2.5cm) fresh ginger root, finely chopped
1 tablespoon garam masala OR curry powder
175g (6oz/¾ cup) red lentils
salt
cayenne pepper
2 tablespoons plain yogurt
fresh cilantro OR mint leaves, to garnish
TO SERVE:
plain yogurt
mini poppadums or warm pita bread
red capsicum and cucumber strips

In a large, heavy-based saucepan over medium heat, heat oil. Add onion, garlic, and ginger and fry for 4-5 minutes until fragrant and onion begins to soften, stirring frequently. Stir in garam masala or curry powder and cook for 1 minute. (See top left.) Add lentils and 2½ cups (20fl oz/ 600ml) cold water. Increase heat and bring to the boil. Cover, reduce heat, and simmer for 30 minutes or until lentils are soft and mash easily when pressed with a spoon against side of pan. (If all the water has not been absorbed, drain well.) Leave to cool.

Reserve about ¼ of lentil mixture. Put remainder into a food processor fitted with a metal blade. Process until smooth, scraping down bowl. Spoon into a serving dish, season with salt and cayenne pepper, and stir in reserved lentils and the yogurt. Cover and refrigerate until required. About 20 minutes before serving, transfer to room temperature. Spoon yogurt on top and sprinkle with cayenne. Garnish, and serve with breads and vegetable strips.

*Serves 6-8*

## CREAMY TAHINI

1 large clove garlic, crushed
115g (4oz/½ cup) sesame seed paste
¼ cup (2fl oz/50ml) Greek-style yogurt
juice 1 lemon
freshly ground black pepper
chopped fresh cilantro OR parsley, to garnish
TO SERVE:
virgin olive oil
raw vegetables
hot pita bread, cut into strips

Rub bottom and side of a shallow serving bowl with garlic then leave garlic in center of bowl.

Add sesame seed paste to bowl; if thick, soften with the back of a wooden spoon. Blend in yogurt, lemon juice, and black pepper. Clean edges of bowl, cover, and refrigerate until ready to serve.

To serve, stir dip again, drizzle virgin olive oil over, and garnish with cilantro or parsley. Serve with a vegetable selection and hot pita strips.

*Serves 6-8*

# CHICKEN SATAY

1lb (450g) boneless, skinless chicken breast, cut into
    1in (2.5cm) strips
sesame seeds, for sprinkling
PEANUT SAUCE:
¼ cup (2oz/50g) smooth or crunchy peanut butter
2-3 tablespoons soy sauce
2 tablespoons sesame oil or vegetable oil
2-3 scallions, chopped
2 cloves garlic, crushed
1in (2.5cm) fresh ginger root, chopped
1 chili, deseeded and chopped
2-3 tablespoons lime juice
1-2 tablespoons brown sugar
MARINADE:
⅓ cup (3fl oz/85ml) vegetable oil
¼ cup (2fl oz/50ml) soy sauce
¼ cup (2fl oz/50ml) lime juice
1in (2.5cm) fresh ginger root, chopped
3-4 cloves of garlic, crushed
1 tablespoon brown sugar
1-2 teaspoons Chinese chili sauce
2 tablespoons chopped fresh cilantro

In a food processor fitted with a metal blade, process all sauce ingredients until smooth, scraping down bowl. If mixture is too stiff, add a little hot water and process again. Spoon into a dipping bowl, cover, and set aside, but not in refrigerator. Put all marinade ingredients into same food processor and process until well blended.

Pour marinade into a shallow dish. Add chicken and turn to coat well. Marinate for 3-4 hours in a cool place, or overnight in the refrigerator. Preheat broiler and line broiler pan with foil. Thread 6in (15cm) skewers with 2 chicken strips, pushing them together. Arrange on pan and sprinkle with sesame seeds. Broil for 5 minutes, turning once, until cooked through and golden brown. Serve hot with sauce and red capsicum and cucumber strips.

*Makes 24*

## PESTO & BEAN DIP

2-3 tablespoon pine nuts
15oz (425g) can cannellini beans, drained and rinsed
¼ cup (2fl oz/50ml) pesto sauce
1-2 tablespoons lemon juice
1-2 cloves garlic, crushed
2 tablespoons virgin olive oil, plus extra to serve
salt and freshly ground black pepper
fresh basil leaves, to garnish
GARLIC CROSTINI:
1 thin loaf French bread
olive oil, for brushing
2 cloves garlic, halved

In a skillet over a medium-low heat, toast pine nuts until golden, tossing frequently. Pour on to a plate to cool.

In a food processor fitted with a metal blade, process beans, pesto, lemon juice, and garlic until smooth, scraping down bowl occasionally. Add olive oil, and salt and pepper and process to blend. If mixture is too stiff, add a little water to thin. Scrape into a bowl, cover, and refrigerate.

To make garlic crostini, preheat oven to 400F (200C). Put bread slices on a baking sheet and brush with olive oil. Bake for about 6 minutes until golden and crisp, turning once. Remove to a wire rack to cool slightly. Rub oiled sides of bread with cut sides of garlic cloves. Arrange on a plate or in a basket. About 1 hour before serving, transfer dip to room temperature. Drizzle with olive oil and sprinkle with basil leaves. Serve with the garlic crostini.

*Serves 4-6*

## SPICY CITRUS SALSA

1 pink grapefruit
1 large orange
1 lime
1 plum tomato, deseeded and chopped (see page 11)
1 clove garlic, finely chopped
1 green chili, peeled, deseeded, and finely chopped
  (see page 11)
2 tablespoons virgin olive oil
1-2 tablespoons raspberry or other fruit vinegar
salt
4 tablespoons chopped fresh chives

Using a sharp knife, slice top and bottom off grapefruit, orange and lemon. Starting at one end, peel the skin and pith from fruit.

Holding grapefruit in one hand and working over a large bowl to catch the juice, slice down between membranes of fruit, twisting to remove segment. Repeat to remove all segments. Squeeze juice from remaining segments and center core. Add to bowl. Prepare orange and lime in the same way. If liked, cut any large grapefruit and orange segments into smaller pieces.

Add tomato, garlic, chili, oil, vinegar, salt, and chives. Stir to blend. Cover and refrigerate until required, preferably no longer than 3-4 hours.

*Serves 6-8*

# APRICOT-MANGO-RADISH SALSA

1 large ripe mango
2-3 ripe apricots
1 bunch (about 12) large red radishes
juice of 1 lime or lemon
1-2 small red chili, deseeded and finely chopped
2-3 tablespoons virgin olive oil
salt
2-3 tablespoons chopped fresh cilantro or mint

Using a large sharp knife, slice down along large center pit of mango removing flesh from both sides. Cut each half vertically in half again. Remove skin by sliding knife between skin and flesh, trimming any stray pieces of skin. Chop into ½in (1cm) pieces. Trim skin from side of pit. Cut away any flesh still clinging to pit, and chop. Put chopped mango and any juices into a large bowl.

Halve apricots, remove pits and chop into ¼in (1cm) pieces. Add to mango with radishes, lime or lemon juice, chili, olive oil, salt, and cilantro or mint. Stir well to blend. Cover and refrigerate for about 2 hours.

*Serves 6-8*

**TIP:** When using fresh mint, do not prepare too far ahead as the herb will darken.

# - PINEAPPLE & AVOCADO SALSA -

1 ripe avocado, pitted (see page 11)
juice of 1 lime
1 pineapple
1 large red onion, finely chopped
1-2 chilies, deseeded and finely chopped
2 sticks celery, finely sliced
1 tablespoon brown sugar
2-3 tablespoons olive oil
2 tablespoons chopped fresh celery leaves, lovage, or
 mint

Scoop flesh from avocado and coarsely chop. Put in a bowl and pour lime juice over; toss gently to coat.

Lay pineapple on a chopping board and, using a large sharp knife, cut off leafy and stem ends. Set on its base and cut away skin. Use a small knife to cut out any remaining eyes. Quarter pineapple and remove core. Chop remaining flesh.

Add pineapple to avocado with onion, chili, celery, brown sugar, and oil. Toss to mix well. Add celery leaves, lovage, or mint. Cover and refrigerate until required.

*Serves 8-10*

**TIP:** Lovage is a herb with a lovely flavor that is somewhere between celery and mint. Grow your own or look out for specialist herb dealers.

# - CHERRY TOMATO & FETA SALSA -

¼ small white, green, or red cabbage
1 cup (4oz/115g) Kalamata or other black olives
2-3 tablespoons red wine vinegar
1lb (450g) cherry tomatoes, halved
1 small cucumber, lightly peeled
8oz (225g) feta cheese, diced
1-2 pickled hot peppers OR fresh chilies, deseeded
  and chopped
⅓-½ cup (3-4fl oz/85-115ml) virgin olive oil
4-6 tablespoons chopped fresh cilantro OR flat-leaf
  parsley

Using a large, sharp knife, quarter cabbage
and remove core. Finely shred cabbage.

With a cherry pitter, remove pits from
olives.

In a large bowl, toss cabbage with vinegar,
cherry tomatoes, and olives. Cut cucumber
lengthwise into quarters and remove seeds.
Chop into ½in (1cm) pieces and add to the
cabbage mixture. Stir in cheese, pickled
peppers or chilies, olive oil, and cilantro or
parsley. Cover and refrigerate for 3-4 hours.

*Serves 10-12*

**TIP:** Pickled hot peppers are available from
supermarkets and Greek specialty stores.

# CHILI-LOVERS' SALSA

4-5 habanero chilies, or other medium-sized hot chili
2 jalapeño chilies, deseeded
2 ripe plum or beefsteak tomatoes, peeled and
    deseeded (see page 11)
2 cloves garlic, finely chopped
1 tablespoon finely chopped onion
2-3 tablespoons olive oil
2 tablespoons red wine vinegar
1 tablespoon light brown sugar
3-4 tablespoons chopped fresh cilantro OR parsley

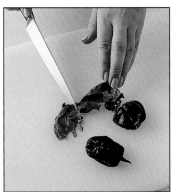

Preheat the broiler. Arrange habanero chilies on a foil-lined broiler pan and broil for about 5 minutes until charred and blistered, turning frequently. Transfer to a large plastic bag, seal top and leave until cool enough to handle. (See top left.) Peel off charred skin and remove stem and seeds. Chop flesh.

Chop both types of chilies and the tomatoes. Put into a medium bowl. Add garlic, onion, olive oil, vinegar, brown sugar, and cilantro or parsley. Stir together. Spoon salsa into a serving bowl, cover, and refrigerate until required.

*Serves 8-10*

# — COCONUT & GRAPE SALSA —

1 small coconut
8oz (225g) fresh lychees
12oz (350g) seedless green grapes, halved
peel and juice of 1 lime
1in (2.5cm) fresh ginger root, chopped
1-2 tablespoons Thai or Italian basil
1-2 teaspoons sugar or honey
1-2 dashes hot pepper sauce
½ teaspoon Thai fish sauce
fine strips of coconut, to garnish

Using a skewer or screwdriver, pierce the 3 'eyes' of the coconut. Drain 'milk' into a cup and reserve for another use. Put coconut into a plastic or freezer bag and twist to close. Place on a stone or brick floor or sturdy surface and strike coconut sharply with a hammer to crack it open. Use a small knife to prize flesh from hairy outer shell. Break flesh into small pieces and grate into a large bowl. (See top right.) Peel and pit lychees.

Add lychees to coconut with grapes, lime peel and juice, ginger, basil, and sugar or honey. Stir together. Season with hot pepper sauce and Thai fish sauce. Spoon into a serving bowl, cover, and refrigerate for about 1 hour. Garnish with coconut strips to serve.

*Serves 8-10*

**TIPS:** If fresh lychees are not available, use a 15oz (425g) can lychees in their own juice (or syrup), drained.

# ─── MINTED MELON SALSA ───

2lb (1kg) watermelon wedge
1 small cantaloupe or other orange-fleshed melon
½ honeydew or pale green-fleshed melon such as Galia
1 orange
1 lime
2 green chilies, deseeded and finely chopped
2 scallions, finely chopped
2 tablespoons olive oil
4 tablespoons chopped fresh mint

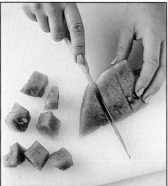

Peel watermelon wedge, remove seeds, and cut flesh into ½in (1cm) cubes. Put into a bowl.

Cut cantaloupe melon into half. Scoop out seeds from cantaloupe melon and honeydew or Galia melon half. Cut flesh into cubes. Add to bowl. Using a vegetable peeler, remove peel from orange and lime, being careful not to remove any bitter white pith. Arrange in stacks of 3-4 strips and, using a sharp knife, cut into very thin julienne strips. Add to melon.

Squeeze juice from orange and lime, add to melon and stir to combine. Add chilies, scallions, olive oil, and mint and toss again until just blended. Cover and refrigerate for 2-3 hours.

*Serves 10-12*

**TIP:** A lemon zester can be used to remove long strips of peel from the orange and lime instead of cutting peel into julienne strips.

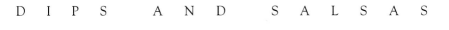

# WARM TOMATO SALSA

4 tablespoons virgin olive oil
1-2 red chilies, deseeded and finely chopped
2 cloves garlic, gently crushed
4-6 large, ripe, full-flavored, tomatoes, peeled,
   deseeded, and coarsely chopped (see page 11)
1 tablespoon capers, rinsed
1 teaspoon chopped fresh thyme OR oregano
1 tablespoon balsamic vinegar OR fruity wine vinegar
1 teaspoon brown sugar
2 tablespoons chopped fresh parsley

In a saucepan over a very low heat, heat
2 tablespoons olive oil, the chilies, and
garlic for 5 minutes until fragrant, stirring.
Cool for about 10 minutes. Discard garlic.

Add tomatoes, capers, thyme or oregano,
vinegar, and brown sugar to pan and stir
gently to combine. Stir in 1 tablespoon
parsley and pour into a serving bowl.

Drizzle remaining olive oil over and sprinkle
with remaining parsley; serve warm.

*Serves 6-8*

## SPICY MANGO DIP

1 large ripe mango
1 tablespoon plum sauce OR hoisin sauce
1½ tablespoons clear honey
1 teaspoon Chinese chili sauce
1 tablespoon cider vinegar OR white wine vinegar
vegetable oil
2 scallions, chopped
1 teaspoon ground cumin
½ teaspoon Chinese five-spice powder
½ teaspoon ground cinnamon
1 tablespoon chopped fresh chives OR cilantro
wontons, to serve

Using a large sharp knife, slice down along large center pit of mango removing flesh from both sides. Cut each half vertically in half again. Remove skin by sliding knife between skin and flesh, trimming any stray pieces of skin. Chop into ½in (1cm) pieces. Trim skin from side of pit. Cut away any flesh still clinging to pit, and chop.

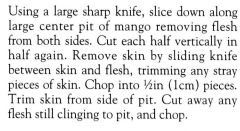

In a food processor fitted with a metal blade, process mango and any juice, plum sauce or hoisin sauce, honey, chili sauce, and vinegar until well blended.

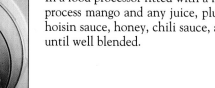

In a skillet over a medium heat, heat 2 tablespoons vegetable oil. Add scallions, cumin, Chinese five-spice powder, and cinnamon and cook for 3-4 minutes until onion is slightly softened and spices are fragrant.

Immediately pour into mango mixture and process until smooth. Pour into a serving bowl and cover until required.

In a large, heavy-based saucepan, or wok, over a medium-high heat, heat 3in (7.5cm) vegetable oil until just beginning to smoke. Add 4-6 wontons and fry for about 3 minutes until golden, turning once. Drain on paper towels and repeat with remaining wontons. Arrange on plate with wooden toothpicks. Sprinkle chives or cilantro over dip and serve with wontons.

*Serves 8-10*

# —APPLE, RAISIN, & MINT SALSA—

½ cup (3oz/85g) raisins
2 large crisp, green apples, such as Granny Smith
1-2 tablespoons lemon juice
1 small mild onion OR 4 scallions, finely chopped
leaves from 1 large bunch fresh mint
1 tablespoon clear honey

In a small bowl, put raisins, cover with boiling water, and leave for 5 minutes to plump. Drain then dry well on paper towels.

Peel apples, if liked, remove cores, and chop. In a medium bowl, toss apples, lemon juice, and onion or scallions together.

Reserve a few mint leaves for garnish. Chop remaining mint very finely. Stir into apple mixture with raisins and honey and stir well. Spoon into a serving bowl and garnish with reserved mint leaves. Serve within 30 minutes.

*Serves 6-8*

# — BLACK BEAN & CORN SALSA —

1½ cups (9oz/250g) sweetcorn kernels
15oz (425g) can black beans, drained and rinsed
1 red onion, finely chopped
1 large red capsicum, finely chopped
2 small red or green chilies, deseeded and finely
  chopped
½ cup (4fl oz/115ml) mayonnaise
¼ cup (2fl oz/50ml) sour cream
1-2 tablespoons white or red wine vinegar
1 teaspoon hot or mild chili powder
½ head Iceberg lettuce, to serve
2 scallions, finely chopped, to garnish

In a bowl, combine sweetcorn, black beans, onion, red capsicum, and chilies.

In a small bowl, whisk together mayonnaise, sour cream, vinegar, and chili powder. Pour over corn and bean mixture and stir to blend well. Cover and refrigerate until required.

To serve, shred lettuce and arrange in a small serving dish. Spoon salsa into center of the lettuce and sprinkle with scallions.

*Serves 8-10*

# – WATERMELON & ONION SALSA –

2lb (1kg) watermelon wedge
1 sweet onion such as Vidalia or Walla Walla, finely
  chopped
1 cup (5oz/150g) canned black beans, drained and
  rinsed
2 jalapeño chilies, deseeded and finely chopped
1 clove garlic, finely chopped
1-2 tablespoons brown sugar
2 tablespoons lemon juice
3-4 tablespoons chopped fresh cilantro OR mint

Using a large knife, peel, deseed, and chop
watermelon.

In a large bowl, combine watermelon,
onion, black beans, chilies, and garlic.

In a small bowl or cup, stir sugar and lemon
juice to dissolve the sugar. Pour over
watermelon mixture, add the cilantro or
mint, and toss together. Spoon into a
serving dish, cover and refrigerate for about
1 hour.

*Serves 10-12*

# GRILLED CORN SALSA

2 large ears sweetcorn, grilled or broiled
1 red or large sweet onion, finely chopped
4 ripe plum tomatoes, deseeded and coarsely chopped
 (see page 11)
1 clove garlic, finely chopped
2 jalapeño chilies, deseeded and finely chopped
leaves from 1 bunch cilantro, finely chopped
salt and freshly ground black pepper

Hold one ear of corn, stem end down, vertically at a slight angle to chopping board. Using a sharp knife, cut down along cob to remove kernels. Place in a large bowl and repeat with remaining corn.

Using the knife, scrape along each cob, removing remaining 'milk' from cobs and add to bowl. Stir in onion.

Add tomatoes, garlic, chilies, cilantro, salt, and pepper. Toss together and spoon into a serving bowl. Allow to stand for about 30 minutes before serving.

*Serves 10-12*

# APRICOT SALSA

6-8 ripe apricots
1 small red onion, finely chopped
1 small red capsicum, deseeded and finely chopped
1 small red chili, deseeded and chopped
1in (2.5cm) fresh ginger root, finely grated
2 tablespoons virgin olive oil
2 tablespoons lime juice
1 tablespoon chopped fresh parsley
soft lettuce leaves, to serve
julienne of lemon peel
coriander (cilantro) leaves

Halve apricots, remove pits and chop into ½in (1cm) pieces. Put into a large bowl; add any excess juices to the bowl.

Add red onion, red capsicum, chili, and ginger and toss well to combine. Drizzle olive oil and lime juice over and add parsley. Stir well to blend. Cover and refrigerate for 1-2 hours.

# CRANBERRY SALSA

1⅓ cups (8oz/225g) fresh or frozen cranberries
⅓-½ cup (3-4oz/85-115g) sugar
2-3 scallions, finely chopped
1 jalapeño chili, deseeded and chopped
1in (2.5cm) fresh ginger root, finely chopped
grated peel and juice of 1-1½ limes
salt
3-4 tablespoons chopped fresh cilantro OR mint

In a food processor fitted with a metal blade, using pulse button, process cranberries and sugar until mixture is coarsely chopped, scraping down bowl once or twice.

Add scallions, chili, ginger, lime peel and juice, and a little salt. Pulse until mixture is evenly chopped, but still has a good texture. Add cilantro or mint and pulse to blend. Scrape into a serving bowl, cover, and refrigerate for 2-3 hours or overnight.

*Serves 4-6*

# —CUCUMBER-CAPSICUM SALSA—

2 large cucumbers
salt
1 red capsicum, deseeded and finely chopped
2 shallots, finely chopped
1 clove garlic, finely chopped
1 red chili, deseeded and finely chopped
2 tablespoons lime juice
2-3 tablespoons extra-virgin olive oil
1-2 teaspoons sugar
4-5 tablespoons chopped fresh dill OR mint

Peel and quarter cucumbers lengthwise; discard seeds. Put cucumbers into a colander, sprinkle with about 2 teaspoons salt and leave to drain for about 40 minutes.

Rinse cucumber pieces and spread on paper towels to dry. Transfer to a large bowl. Add red capsicum, shallots, garlic, and chili, and toss to combine.

In a small bowl, stir lime juice, olive oil, and sugar to dissolve sugar. Pour over cucumber mixture, cover, and refrigerate for about 1 hour. Stir in dill or mint, then spoon into a serving dish.

*Serves 6-8*

**TIP:** Thin-skinned cucumbers do not need peeling, but varieties with a thick skin, which is often waxed for a shiny presentation, do need to be peeled.

# HERB SALSA

1 small red onion, finely chopped
1-2 sticks celery, with leaves, if possible, finely
  chopped
1 cup (1oz/25g) chopped fresh herbs such as parsley,
  cilantro, mint, dill, oregano, or thyme
2-3 tablespoons lime OR lemon juice
1 teaspoon light brown sugar
½-1 teaspoon cayenne pepper
salt

In a glass or other non-corrosive bowl, stir together onion, celery, and chopped fresh herbs.

Add lime or lemon juice, brown sugar, cayenne pepper, and salt. Toss together. Cover and refrigerate for about 1 hour. Spoon into a serving dish.

*Serves 6-8*

**TIP:** This salsa is delicious stirred into a vegetable soup just before serving. Alternatively, stir into yogurt or sour cream and serve as a dip.

# WARM SALSA VERDE

2-3 jalapeño chilies, deseeded and coarsely chopped
6-8 scallions, coarsely chopped
1-2 cloves garlic, crushed
⅓ cup (2oz/50g) capers, rinsed
1 bunch fresh parsley
½ bunch fresh tarragon, dill, cilantro OR mint
1 cup (8fl oz/225ml) extra-virgin olive oil
finely grated peel and juice of 1 large lemon
salt
julienne of lemon peel, to garnish

In a food processor fitted with a metal blade, process chilies, scallions, and garlic until blended, scraping down the side of the bowl once or twice. Add capers and herbs, and, using pulse button, process until finely chopped. In a medium saucepan over a low heat, heat olive oil until just warm. Stir in herb mixture and immediately remove pan from heat.

Add lemon peel and juice, and season with a little salt. Serve warm garnished with lemon peel julienne.

*Serves 6-8*

# - MANGO-PASSION-FRUIT SALSA -

⅓ cup (3oz/85g) sultanas
1 large ripe mango
2-4 passion-fruit, halved
1 sweet onion such as Vidalia or Walla Walla, or red
   onion, finely chopped
grated peel and juice of 1 lime
2 tablespoons chopped fresh mint
salt
2-3 dashes hot pepper sauce

Put sultanas in a small bowl and cover with boiling water. Leave for 5 minutes to plump. Drain and dry well on paper towels.

Using a large sharp knife, slice down along large center pit of mango removing flesh from both sides. Cut each half vertically in half again. Remove skin by sliding knife between skin and flesh, trimming any stray pieces of skin. Chop into ½in (1cm) pieces. Trim skin from side of pit. Cut away any flesh still clinging to pit, and chop. Put chopped mango and any juices into a large bowl.

Using a spoon, scoop pulp and seeds from passion-fruit. Put into bowl with mango, raisins, onion, lime peel and juice, the mint, and salt. Sprinkle over a few dashes of hot pepper sauce. Toss and stir gently to blend. Spoon into a serving dish, cover, and refrigerate for about 30 minutes.

*Serves 8-10*

**TIP:** Look for the most shriveled and wrinkled passion-fruit because this is a sign of ripeness.

# —COCONUT & APPLE SALSA—

flesh of 1 small coconut (see page 63)
4 crisp, green apples such as Granny Smith, peeled, if
    liked
1 small onion, finely chopped
1 small red chili, deseeded and chopped OR
    ½ teaspoon dried crushed chili flakes
4 tablespoons lime juice
1 tablespoon clear honey
salt
½ cup (1½oz/40g) shredded unsweetened coconut
2 tablespoons chopped fresh mint OR cilantro

Grate coconut flesh and add to a large bowl.

Core and finely chop apples. Add to coconut with onion and chili or chili flakes and toss to blend.

In a small bowl, stir lime juice, honey, and salt to dissolve salt. Pour over coconut and apple mixture and stir in unsweetened shredded coconut and the mint or cilantro. Spoon into a serving dish and leave for 15 minutes before serving. Garnish with thin coconut slices, if liked.

*Serves 10-12*

# — PEACH & NECTARINE SALSA —

3 ripe peaches
3 ripe nectarines
1 small red or yellow capsicum, deseeded and
  chopped
1 small red onion, finely chopped
1 red chili, deseeded and finely chopped
1in (2.5cm) fresh ginger root, finely grated
1 piece stem ginger in syrup, chopped
1 tablespoon ginger syrup
2-3 tablespoons lime OR lemon juice
½ teaspoon ground cumin
½ teaspoon ground coriander
2 tablespoons chopped fresh cilantro
2 tablespoons chopped fresh mint

Remove pits from peaches and nectarines. Cut flesh into approximately ¼in (5mm) pieces and put into a large bowl. Add red or yellow capsicum, onion, chili, fresh ginger, stem ginger, and ginger syrup. Mix together.

In a small bowl, stir together lime or lemon juice, cumin, and ground coriander. Stir in the peach mixture with cilantro and mint. Spoon into a serving dish, cover, and refrigerate for about 1 hour.

*Serves 10-12*

**TIP:** Stem ginger in syrup combines the hot ginger flavor and the sweetness of the syrup, and is wonderful in fruit salads and desserts. It can be found in specialist food stores and some supermarkets.

# — PINEAPPLE & PAPAYA SALSA —

1 pineapple
1 papaya
½ cucumber, lightly peeled, deseeded, and chopped
2-3 scallions, finely chopped
1-2 small red chilies, sliced on the diagonal
2-3 tablespoons lemon OR lime juice
1 tablespoon clear honey
½ cup (2oz/50g) salted peanuts, coarsely chopped
2-3 tablespoons chopped fresh cilantro OR mint

Trim pineapple, cut away skin and cut out any remaining eyes (see page 60). Quarter pineapple and remove core. Chop remaining flesh.

Peel papaya and cut in half lengthwise. Scoop out dark seeds. Chop flesh into ¼in (5mm) pieces. Put into a bowl.

Add pineapple, cucumber, scallions, chilies, lemon or lime juice, honey, peanuts, and cilantro or mint to bowl. Stir well to combine and spoon into a serving dish. Cover and refrigerate for about 30 minutes.

*Serves 8-10*

# PEAR SALSA

2 large, ripe dessert pears, about 1lb (450g), cored
  and cut into ½in (1cm) cubes
2 dried pear halves, cut into ¼in (5mm) pieces
½ cucumber, peeled, deseeded, and chopped
½ small red onion, chopped
grated peel and juice of 1 lime
1in (2.5cm) fresh ginger root, finely chopped
1 piece stem ginger in syrup, finely chopped
1 tablespoon ginger syrup
1 jalapeño chili, deseeded and finely chopped
2 tablespoons chopped fresh mint
salt

In a large bowl, combine pears, dried pears,
cucumber, red onion, and lime peel and
juice.

Stir in fresh ginger, stem ginger and syrup,
chili, mint, and a little salt. Spoon into a
serving bowl, cover, and refrigerate for no
longer than 1 hour.

*Serves 8-10*

# — BERRY MASCARPONE SWIRL —

1lb (450g) fresh blueberries, raspberries, and
  chopped strawberries
1 tablespoon sugar
½ teaspoon ground cinnamon
2 teaspoons arrowroot
1 tablespoon lemon juice
½ cup (4oz/115g) mascarpone cheese, softened
½ cup (4fl oz/115ml) heavy cream OR thick plain
  yogurt
fresh mint sprigs, to garnish
sliced fruit such as apples, pears, bananas, mangoes,
  pineapples, peaches, nectarines, to serve

In a medium, heavy-based saucepan over a
medium-high heat, bring fruit, sugar,
cinnamon, and 2 tablespoons water to the
boil then simmer for 2-3 minutes until fruit
is completely softened. In a small bowl, stir
arrowroot with lemon juice to dissolve.
Slowly whisk into berry mixture, which will
thicken immediately. Remove from heat
and leave to cool completely, stirring
occasionally to prevent a skin forming. Pour
into a bowl, cover, and refrigerate until
required.

In a medium bowl, stir together mascarpone
cheese and cream or yogurt. Spoon into a
shallow serving bowl. Gently stir in berry
mixture to create a swirl or marbled pattern.
Garnish with a mint sprig and serve with
sliced fruits.

*Serves 4-6*

# CHOCOLATE FONDUE

8oz (225g) good quality bittersweet chocolate,
  chopped
1-2 tablespoons golden syrup OR corn syrup
  (optional)
¾ cup (6fl oz/175ml) heavy cream
2-3 tablespoons brandy, orange liqueur, OR amaretto
mixed fruits such as cherries, seedless grapes, Cape
  gooseberries, strawberries, sliced bananas, figs,
  mango, and clementine segments, to serve

In a medium, heavy-based saucepan over a
medium-low heat, heat chocolate, golden or
corn syrup, if using, and cream, stirring until
melted and completely smooth.

Remove from heat and stir in brandy or
liqueur. Pour into a small fondue pot set
over a candle burner to keep warm.
Alternatively pour into a small heatproof
serving bowl. Arrange a selection of fruits
on a serving plate in an attractive pattern.
Serve with fondue and fondue forks or
wooden toothpicks.

*Serves 6-8*

**TIP:** Brush banana, pear, or apple slices
with lemon juice to prevent darkening.

# - CRANBERRY & ORANGE RELISH -

1 orange, preferably seedless
1 lemon
1 lime
1lb (450g) fresh cranberries
1½ cups (12oz/350g) sugar, plus extra, if needed
2 tablespoons chopped fresh mint (optional)

Grate peel from orange, lemon, and lime. Carefully peel bitter white pith from each fruit and cut flesh into quarters. In a food processor fitted with a metal blade, using pulse button, process cranberries until coarsely chopped.

Add fruit peels to cranberries with sugar, and mint, if using. Pulse until mixture is well chopped but still has an even texture. Taste and add more sugar if necessary. Scrape into a bowl, cover, and refrigerate overnight to blend flavors.

*Serves 10-12*

**TIP:** The relish will keep for 2 weeks refrigerated or can be frozen for up to 6 months.

# ──ROAST CAPSICUM RELISH──

1 large red capsicum
1 large yellow capsicum
1 large green capsicum
1 large jalapeño OR other medium chili, peeled,
  deseeded, and chopped (see page 11)
1 small red onion, finely chopped
1-2 cloves garlic, finely chopped
2 tablespoons extra-virgin olive oil, plus extra for
  brushing
1-2 tablespoons balsamic vinegar
2 tablespoons shredded fresh basil
salt and freshly ground black pepper

Preheat broiler. Arrange capsicums on a
foil-lined broiler pan or baking sheet and
broil for 8-10 minutes until charred and
blistered, turning frequently. Transfer to a
plastic bag, twist to seal the top, and leave
until the peppers are cool enough to handle.
Alternatively, transfer charred capsicums to
a chopping board and cover with a large
inverted bowl. Peel off charred skin and
remove the stem and seeds. Chop flesh
reserving any juices.

Put capsicums and chili into a bowl with
their juices. Stir in onion, garlic, olive oil,
balsamic vinegar, basil, and salt and black
pepper. Cover and refrigerate for about
2 hours or until required.

*Serves 6-8*

# SPICY HAMBURGER RELISH

3 tablespoons olive oil
1 onion, finely chopped
1 red capsicum, chopped
2-3 cloves garlic, finely chopped
1in (2.5cm) fresh ginger root, finely chopped
6 large ripe tomatoes, peeled and cut into ½in (1cm)
　pieces (see page 11)
1 teaspoon dried chili flakes
1 teaspoon ground cinnamon
1 teaspoon ground nutmeg
salt and freshly ground black pepper
⅓ cup (3fl oz/85ml) balsamic vinegar OR cider
　vinegar
⅓ cup (3oz/85g) light OR dark brown sugar
1-2 tablespoons chopped fresh cilantro OR parsley

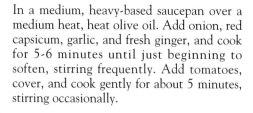

In a medium, heavy-based saucepan over a medium heat, heat olive oil. Add onion, red capsicum, garlic, and fresh ginger, and cook for 5-6 minutes until just beginning to soften, stirring frequently. Add tomatoes, cover, and cook gently for about 5 minutes, stirring occasionally.

Stir in chili flakes, cinnamon, nutmeg, salt and pepper, vinegar, and sugar and bring to the boil, stirring to dissolve sugar. Simmer for about 20 minutes until liquid has evaporated and vegetables are tender. Remove from heat and stir in cilantro or parsley. Set aside to cool. Pour into a glass or plastic container with an airtight cover and refrigerate for up to 1 week.

*Serves 12-14*

# HOISIN RELISH

½ cup (4fl oz/115ml) hoisin sauce OR Chinese plum
   sauce
¼ cup (2fl oz/50ml) tomato catsup
2 tablespoons Japanese soy sauce
2 tablespoons Chinese chili sauce
2-4 scallions, thinly sliced diagonally
1in (2.5cm) piece of fresh ginger root, finely grated
fresh cilantro leaves, to garnish
asparagus spears, baby sweetcorn, or cucumber strips,
   for dipping

Put hoisin sauce or plum sauce in a bowl
and blend in catsup, soy sauce, and chili
sauce. If too thick, add a little hot water to
thin to a dipping consistency.

Stir in scallions and ginger. Spoon into a
serving bowl, cover and refrigerate for about
30 minutes or until required. Garnish with a
few cilantro leaves before serving.

*Serves 6-8*

**TIP:** Hoisin sauce is made from soy flour,
chilies, ginger, garlic, and sugar. Plum sauce
is prepared from plums, apricots, garlic,
chilies, sugar, and vinegar. Both can be
found in supermarkets or Chinese groceries.

# —ROAST GARLIC MAYONNAISE —

2 unpeeled bulbs garlic, separated into cloves
extra-virgin olive oil
1 cup good-quality mayonnaise
1 tablespoon Dijon mustard
1 tablespoon white wine vinegar OR  lemon juice
salt
cayenne pepper

Preheat oven to 350F (180C). Put garlic cloves into a small roasting pan and drizzle with 2-3 tablespoons olive oil, toss well to coat evenly. Roast for 35-40 minutes, stirring occasionally, until very tender when pierced with the tip of a knife.

Transfer to a plate to cool, then squeeze each garlic clove out of its skin into a food processor fitted with metal blade. Process until smooth, scraping the side of the bowl once or twice. Add mayonnaise, mustard, vinegar or lemon juice, and process to blend. Season with a little salt and cayenne pepper.

With the machine running, gradually add about ½ cup (4fl oz/115ml) of the oil in a thin steady stream, until oil is incorporated and mayonnaise is thick and creamy. Add more salt and cayenne pepper if necessary. If not using immediately, add about 2 tablespoons boiling water and process to blend; this helps prevent mayonnaise from separating when refrigerated. Cover and refrigerate for up to 3 days. To serve, bring to room temperature and stir.

*Serves 8-10*

# — AVOCADO-TOMATO RELISH —

2 'balls' fresh buffalo mozzarella in water, about 4oz
    (115g) each, drained
4 ripe plum tomatoes
1 ripe avocado
2 tablespoons sun-dried tomatoes in oil, drained and
    chopped
1 small red chili, deseeded and thinly sliced
salt and freshly ground black pepper
2 tablespoons shredded fresh basil
2 tablespoons extra-virgin olive oil
1-2 tablespoons balsamic vinegar

Pat mozzarella dry with paper towels. Chop
into ½in (1cm) pieces and transfer to a large
bowl.

With a small sharp knife cut off stem end of
tomatoes, and score rounded end. Lower
into boiling water and leave for 30-60
seconds until skin begins to curl off flesh.
Drain, rinse under running cold water and
drain again. Using a small sharp knife, or
your fingertips, peel off the skins. Halve
tomatoes lengthwise. Squeeze out seeds or
use a spoon to scoop out seeds and liquid.
Cut into ¼in (5mm) pieces.

With a sharp knife, cut avocado in half.
Twist halves apart and remove pit by
striking with the blade of the knife and
twisting out. Using a spoon, scoop out flesh
and chop. Add tomatoes, avocado, sun-
dried tomatoes, chili, basil, and salt and
pepper to mozzarella. Drizzle olive oil over
and toss lightly to combine. Spoon into a
serving bowl and drizzle with balsamic
vinegar. Serve within 30 minutes otherwise
the avocado will darken.

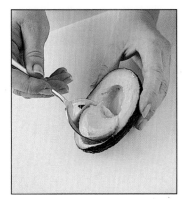

*Serves 8-10*

# —— FETA & TOMATO RELISH ——

8oz (225g) feta cheese, crumbled or chopped
1½ cups (6oz/175g) Kalamata olives, pitted and halved
8oz (225g) cherry tomatoes, deseeded and quartered
1-2 cloves garlic, finely chopped
1 small red chili, deseeded and chopped
1 tablespoon capers, rinsed and drained
2-3 tablespoons coarsely chopped fresh flat-leaf parsley
1 tablespoon chopped fresh oregano
3 tablespoons olive oil
1-2 tablespoons red wine OR balsamic vinegar
½ teaspoon sugar
salt and freshly ground black pepper
1 large bulb fennel, halved lengthwise

Put feta and olives into a large bowl and toss together.

Add tomatoes, garlic, chili, capers, parsley, oregano, 2 tablespoons olive oil, the vinegar, sugar,
 and pepper to feta-olive mixture and stir gently to combine. Add salt if necessary.

Core and thinly slice fennel. Toss with remaining olive oil; season with a little pepper. Spread on a serving dish and top with relish. Serve within 30 minutes, or cover and refrigerate until chilled.

*Serves 6-8*

# ―― RED ONION MARMALADE ――

2 tablespoons olive oil
2 large red onions, thinly sliced
1 tablespoon light brown sugar
1 sprig fresh thyme OR ½ teaspoon dried thyme
1-2 tablespoons balsamic OR raspberry vinegar
1-2 teaspoons butter
1-2 tablespoons chopped fresh parsley
12-16 black olives (preferably Kalamata or Niçoise),
   halved and pitted

In a medium, heavy-based skillet over a medium heat, heat olive oil. Add red onions and cook over a medium-low heat for about 10 minutes until softened, stirring frequently; do not allow to brown otherwise they may taste bitter.

Stir in sugar, thyme, vinegar, and butter and cook for 10 minutes more until very soft and glazed. Add 1-2 teaspoons water if mixture is too dry or begins to brown. Stir in parsley and olives. Remove from heat and leave to cool. Serve warm, or cover and refrigerate for up to 1 week.

*Serves 6-8*

# -CAPSICUM & KUMQUAT RELISH-

2 yellow capsicums, deseeded and finely chopped
225g (8oz) kumquats, quartered and deseeded
115g (4oz) yellow cherry tomatoes
grated peel and juice 1 orange
grated peel and juice 1 lime
1 teaspoon sugar
1 small green chili, deseeded and chopped
1 small bunch fresh chives, chopped
2 tablespoons chopped fresh mint OR basil

Put chopped yellow capsicums and quartered kumquats into a bowl.

Halve and deseed cherry tomatoes; coarsely chop some tomatoes, if liked. Add to bowl with orange and lime peels and juices, sugar, chili, chives, and mint or basil.

Stir well. Spoon into a serving dish, cover and refrigerate for at least 1-2 hours or until required.

*Serves 8-10*

# PAPAYA & PASSION-FRUIT RELISH

2 large carrots, chopped
2 large ripe papaya, peeled, deseeded and chopped
  (see page 80)
1 small red onion, chopped
1 small green or red chili, deseeded and chopped
16oz (450g) can sweetcorn kernels, drained
finely grated peel and juice 1 lime
½ teaspoon coriander seeds, lightly crushed
2 ripe passion-fruit, halved crosswise
2 tablespoons chopped fresh mint
salt and freshly ground black pepper

In a pan of boiling water, simmer carrots for 2 minutes. Drain, rinse under running cold water, drain and pat dry on paper towels.

Transfer carrots to a large bowl. Add papaya, red onion, chili, sweetcorn kernels, lime peel and juice, and coriander seeds. Toss together.

Scoop pulp and seeds from passion-fruit and add to papaya mixture with mint, and salt and pepper. Stir well to combine. Spoon into a serving dish, cover, and refrigerate for 1-2 hours or until required.

*Serves 10-12*

# – PEACH-POMEGRANATE RELISH –

5 ripe peaches
50g (2oz/½ cup) slivered almonds, lightly toasted
finely grated peel and juice of 1 lemon
1 tablespoon pomegranate syrup OR rosewater
1 tablespoon small fresh mint leaves
1 large, ripe pomegranate

Peel peaches (see page 11), remove pits and coarsely chop flesh. Put into a bowl with almonds, lemon peel and juice, pomegranate syrup or rosewater, and mint leaves.

Using your thumbs, pull pomegranate apart from seed end and break into sections. Alternatively, cut lengthwise through with a knife and break apart. Scoop out seeds and remove white pith. Add seeds and juice to bowl.

Toss all ingredients in bowl to combine. Spoon into a serving dish and allow to stand for about 30 minutes before serving.

*Serves 8-10*

**TIP:** Pomegranate syrup and rosewater are available in some larger supermarkets and most Greek or Middle Eastern groceries.

# — SPICY CRANBERRY CHUTNEY —

300g (10oz/2 cups) cranberries
2 packed cups (1lb/450g) light brown sugar
1⅓ cups (11fl oz/325ml) raspberry vinegar OR red
  wine vinegar
2 large red onions, finely chopped
1 red chili, deseeded and finely chopped
1lb (450g) seedless black grapes
1in (2.5cm) fresh ginger root, finely chopped or
  grated
1 teaspoon juniper berries, lightly crushed
seeds from 6-8 cardamom pods
½ teaspoon ground cloves OR allspice
freshly ground black pepper

In a large saucepan over a medium-high
heat, bring cranberries and ¼ cup (2fl oz/
50ml) water to the boil. Cook until
cranberries begin to pop, stirring frequently.

Add sugar and vinegar, reduce heat to
medium and stir until sugar has dissolved.
Stir in remaining ingredients and simmer
gently, uncovered, for about 45 minutes
until mixture is thick and soft. Remove from
heat and leave to cool. Spoon into a serving
bowl and put in refrigerator until required.

*Serves 10-12*

**TIP:** For longer storage, the hot dip can be
bottled in sterilized jars, sealed, and kept for
6 months, or frozen for up to 6 months.

# INDEX